# The Bears Upstairs

*by Jane Belk Moncure*
*illustrated by Sue Knipper,*
*Creative Studios I, Inc.*

Published by  THE CHILD'S WORLD

**Mankato, Minnesota**

## The Library —
## A Magic Castle

*Come to the magic castle*
*When you are growing tall.*
*Rows upon rows of Word Windows*
*Line every single wall.*
*They reach up high,*
*As high as the sky,*
*And you want to open them all.*
*For every time you open one,*
*A new adventure has begun.*

Katie opens a Word Window.
Guess what she sees?

Stairs,

lots

of

stairs.

"I will go upstairs," she says.
Guess what Katie finds upstairs?

Bears,
lots
of
bears.

"Come and play," say the bears.
So Katie finds . . .

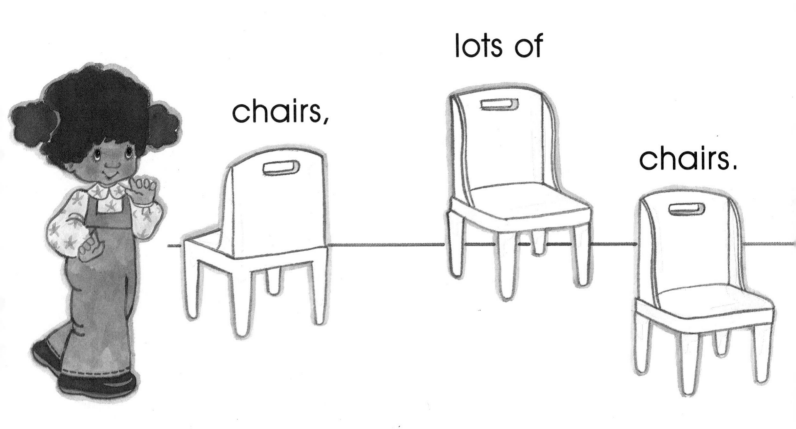

lots of

chairs,

chairs.

"I will make something for the
bears," she says. She makes a . . .

boat out of
chairs for the
bears.

"Let's sail away," say the bears.

The bears make the chairs

go up

and down.

"I like to float in my little chair boat,"
each one says.

But after a while, one bear asks,
"What else can we play today?"

"I know," says Katie.

She makes an airplane out of
chairs for the bears.

"Let's fly high
in the air,"
says a bear.

So away they go.

"What else can we play today?"
ask the bears.

"Make a long line with your chairs,"
says Katie. "Now we have . . .

a train. Here we go down the track,
all the way to town . . .

and back.
Toot! Toot!

choo choo choo choo

Here we go. Fast. Slow. Stop."

"Now what else can we play with our chairs?" ask the bears.

Katie makes
a bus out
of chairs
for the bears.

The bears sing a funny song as
they bump along in their chairs.

They bump . . .

up and down

on the bus.

The bears bump

right out of their chairs
and tumble to the floor.

"Oh, dear, my poor bears," says Katie.

Katie makes a hospital out of chairs
for the bears.

She takes care of each little bear.
"Please don't cry," she says.

Katie

runs

downstairs . . .

and finds yellow pears for the bears.

She shares the pears with the bears.

Then Katie makes a big bed out of chairs for the bears.

She hugs each bear, and says, "Good night." Then . . .

she tiptoes

down

the

stairs . . .

and closes the Word Window.
"I'll be back someday to play
with my bears upstairs," she says.

# Can you read these words with Katie?

chairs

bears

boat

float

upstairs

downstairs

play

today